A CHILD AND A MONSTER

Sharon Griffin Captain

PublishAmerica
Baltimore

First printing

PublishAmerica has allowed this work to remain exactly as the author intended, verbatim, without editorial input.

Hardcover 978-1-4512-9547-4
Softcover 978-1-4489-4363-0
PAperback 978-1-4512-4249-2
Pocketbook 978-1-4489-1610-8
PUBLISHED BY PUBLISHAMERICA, LLLP
www.publishamerica.com
Baltimore

Printed in the United States of America

DISCLAIMER

This book is based on a true story. In order to maintain anonymity, however, all characters in this book are fictitious, and any resemblance to real persons, living or dead, is coincidental.

This book is dedicated to my grandparents on my father's side of the family, for whom I thank God every day. If not for them, I honestly think I would not be here. This book also is dedicated to my two beautiful daughters, my husband, sister, my brother, and my youngest sister who is there for me every step, and my therapist who inspired me to write this book and to help others. They have restored my faith in love and the true meaning of family.

ACKNOWLEDGMENTS

A Message from Lynda

I do not remember much as a young child growing up. I was told by doctors that I blocked a lot of it out. Some of what I do remember is that my sister was terrorized by a woman they called my mother. I like to say she was not a mother she gave birth to me and that is it.

Although my sister was brutally beaten, starved, and mentally abused one of the things I will never forget when I was very young my sister was locked in a closet for what I thought was days without any food or water. I would try to sneak whatever I could to her. When I would ask my sister if she is alright, she would simply reply "yes I am ok" and then she would say to me "are you ok". She would always watch over me and make sure I was not harmed, even if it meant she would be the one to take the abuse. She always protected me no matter what the consequences.

The worst part of the life I endured was watching, hearing, and feeling what was happening to my sister. Why I say this is that I could not do anything to help her get away from that woman.

In my own opinion, I feel that our entire family was to blame. They all knew about what was going on. However, not one person tried to stop her from hurting my sister. This includes aunts, uncles, grandparents, and worst of all; my father (whom I thought was my hero).

I think that I have finally forgiven myself for not being able to help her. She is a woman who has a deep inner strength that would not let her give up.

I hope that this will help others that are being abused and those who know of abuse to speak up.

USE YOUR VOICE PEOPLE

Sis you are an amazing mother, woman, and most of all you are my best friend.

With all my love, Lynda

A Message from Autumn
To My Beautiful Mom'.

I thank the Angels who held you at this time in your life... I thank them because they gave you the faith to survive during your daily fear and wonder, as an innocent child, if there was a nicer world out there... they helped you and guided you to find the final freedom of happiness in falling in love with a wonderful man and father, to give life to two beautiful daughters.

May you know... you are the most loving, caring, strongest woman I have ever grown to know. You are a wonderful... daughter, sister, niece, granddaughter, aunt, sister-in-law, wife, mother, mother-in-law, grandmother, and friend. You have this unique way about you that is loved by others... I love your artistic talent, your imagination and your passion for music. You are free spirited, intelligent, artistic, and creative and fun!

My favorite lessons as a child that I captured from you are the simplest ones in life... and the most important. You taught me how to have fun, live, dance and never give up. You taught me how to care, not judge, and to forgive. I will always hold these simple life lessons dear to my heart as I use them every day and pass them on to my son, your grandson.

Thank you for your strength... I am so proud that you are my Mom and I am so proud of the family I come from and who I am.

May your soul be liberated from all your pain... and may you find peace within your heart.

Thank you for being you. Thank you for being my Mom

A Message from Kristen

I am very proud my mother decided to tell her story. I know it was a very hard thing for her to do, but it has helped her face everything that has happened to her. When I hear what she has gone through, I realize how much strength she truly has.

Her story shines a light on child abuse. Child abuse is something we should never ignore. If you know anyone that is being abused, you should report it. It is wrong to turn your back.

Getting involved is helping the child or in some cases saving the child's life. Many children are afraid to speak up and tell. You can be the voice for that child.

Kristen

A Message from Debbie

I truly never understood the meaning of friendship until I met Sharon. Although we have only known each other a few years she has become my dearest, closest friend. She is the most loving, caring, sharing person I have had the privilege to know.

It is so hard for me to imagine the horrible abuse she endured as a child. I know she is reminded of it every day but she always has something positive to share with me and or her co-workers if only her contagious laughter.

I sincerely hope she can have peace in her life now that she has expressed herself in this book. She deserves that and so much more.

Debbie

A Message from RB

Since both of my parents were abusive I have found it very difficult to trust people. I was unable in my youth to find someone to confide in or get help from. Currently I am in my fifties and I have been through years of therapy as an adult. Try as I may to heal my wounds the effects of abuse still Linger.

RB

A Message from Sharon

For years this book has been hidden, a secret in a wealthy family, a secret inside a child victim that was struggling to come out. Sharing this secret has helped my healing process, but I will never forgive the abuse. Perhaps this book can help other abusers and witnesses of abuse realize how devastating the horror of abuse can be. At first this book was written as therapy, but after researching the nature of abuse and learning more and more about the many helpless children who are suffering similar abuse today, it was decided to share that story.

Hopefully this book and others like it can make a difference. Please always be aware of the children around you and how they are treated. Do not be afraid to reach out and get involved. You could be saving a life. Most importantly, remember that children are defenseless and want approval and love even from their abuser. They are very confused. Some think they are bad children and should be punished this way. One thing is certain; the adults that experienced the same crime as children need to face what they have gone through. You can rest assure that the results of their own abuse are seen in their live as adults. Abused children often grow up to be abusers of children themselves. They may adjust to the abuse, rationalizing it as defense and carrying it forward like anything else they were taught as children. They develop the same rage inside because no one out there ever got involved and reached out to help them when they were abused children. Now as an adult, they still need to be saved.

In my case, my grandparents were there. They showed me that the behavior inflicted on me was not normal. I am grateful to them for doing what they could for me. I do wonder why my grandparents let this abuse stay a secret. The rest of my family, just watched, and did nothing to stop the abuse or even report it to the authorities. This is so unforgivable, and their behavior or lack of it will never cease to be intensely disturbing to me.

I used nonphysical punishments on my own children. I did try spanking them twice. However, I just felt so bad and sick inside that I never could again. I don't believe it is right to hit a child because, it teaches them to hit and that learning can lead to nothing but problems later on for them and their children.

The key to healing from child abuse is to take the time for you. There are many ways to reach out for help. There is a light at the end of this nightmare.

Sharon

Contents

INTRODUCTION

The contents in this book are memories. The events described have happened repeatedly over the years. I have tried to list them chronologically as much as possible. I have been told that it is likely I blocked out the worst abuse, but may remember it as time passes.

THE AUTHOR'S DEFINITIONS OF CHILD ABUSE

Physical Abuse:

Physical abuse occurs when an adult purposefully injures a child or when the child's injuries are inconsistent with the history the adult gives to others regarding the injuries. This kind of abuse includes injuries that can range from minor bruises and lacerations to severe physiological trauma and death. Physically abusive acts can range from unreasonably severe corporal punishment to actual deliberate assault on a child. There are new laws that do protect children from parental corporal punishment, but it is still up to the public to report such abuse.

Emotional Neglect as Abuse:

The emotional neglect component of abuse is the withholding or failure to provide the love, support, and attention necessary for the child's natural emotional and physical development. The emotional abuse component occurs when chronic behavior patterns engaged in by an adult interfere with the psychological and social development of a child or adolescent. Emotionally abusive behavior patterns can include: Rejecting or refusing to accept the child, as well as ignoring or being psychologically unavailable to the child.

Belittling the child's abilities, self-worth and undermining his or her self-confidence with derogatory statements; terrorizing the child through making threatening, humiliating comments.

A sibling child who witnesses the abuse of another child is also being abused.

Sexual Abuse:

The involvement of a child or adolescent in forced, exploitative, or coercive sexual activities controlled by an adult. Abusive sexual activities include both those involving actual physical contact, such as genital or anal contact, as well as sexual offenses without physical contact, such as exhibitionism, verbal sexual comments, and engaging the child in pornography. Sexual abusive acts include humiliating a child sexually by involving the child in exhibitionist acts on themselves.

MEMORIES OF BEING
TWO YEARS OLD

Father's lady friend is smiling at me. Father likes her. She is so pretty and seems so nice.

My grandparents told me the story of my real mom. She had to move far away to England.

There are many flashes of memories that occur from this age. Some are quite distinct and terrifying, bringing images of beatings with a belt across all parts of the body. I can remember feeling my ears feeling on fire and not being able to breathe. Some memories are just an empty feeling. Some of the memories are those of sexual abuse, but not to the point of having a vivid memory of an actual incident.

That lady just gave me a scary look. I hope she likes me.

PICK UP THE FLOOR

CHAPTER ONE

My Father's lady friend was now my stepmother. Father was a pilot and had to go to work often. At times, he was away for days or weeks or even months. Mother would give me that abusive, scary look and say, "You wait, little girl," or "I will teach you, little girl" My stomach would turn over, and I would feel terrified.

I knew what was going to happen next, so I moved down on the floor, and protected myself as best I could…

The door would close again, and my Father would be gone. Mother looked at me with that familiar glare, as she walked towards me, I was shaking so much inside I could barely stand it. Then she would kick me in the stomach and ribs, three times, so hard I could not breathe. My arms went down, but they were useless and they just got in the way. It hurt so much. Mother had on her black—pointed shoes that she always wore. Feeling the direct hit of her first kick, I could not breathe. All I wanted was to take a deep breath. I knew there were more kicks to come, but I just could not brace myself.

Mother would grab me by the hair and fling me around and say, "Pick up that floor!" That meant I was to get on my hands and knees and pick up every little speck of dirt from the rug for hours. I was happy doing that, because while I did it, she would leave me alone. Even if my knees were sore after a while, it was better than what might come instead.

I could see Mother out of the corner of my eye, and I would never stop peeking to see what she was doing. I picked at each section of the rug, maybe two inches at a time, making sure that every little piece of fuzz was gathered. I would get a handful of fuzz after about an hour, but I did not dare ask to throw it away. I would ball it up in the palm of my hand. My mind would wander too… how long would my Father be gone this time?

I always tried to stay out of sight and be unseen and quiet. My knees were sore, and I was tired and thirsty. I would forget to get a drink before Father went to work, and Mother would not let me have a drink, sometimes for days. If I got to go to the bathroom by myself, I would sneak a drink really quietly just barely turning on the faucet and letting the water drizzle into my mouth. I would often think about the wet water in my mouth and dream about it going down my throat. Then I wanted to go to the bathroom. I had learned how to endure the pain of holding everything in.

I was still in the same t-shirt from the morning and still on my knees. It was getting dark now and I felt so tired. Mother was on the couch reading a book. I Thought, *Oh God, I hope she falls asleep so I can lie down and close my eyes!* I had to go to the bathroom too. I could feel the urge so strongly. But I was too afraid to ask. Finally my lips just burst with a quick and frightened question.

"Can I go to the bathroom?"

The answer was a snarled. "Hurry up, you little bitch!" She'd glare at me with mean black eyes. I would then hurry to the bathroom, but I did not know what to do first— sneak water or sit on the toilet. I relieved my pain first and hurried to the faucet and gulped as much as I could as fast as I could. Then, quietly, I went back out to the living room.

Mother looked up and said again, "Pick up the floor!" I think she was too absorbed in her book to get up. I was relieved and continued to pick up the floor. Finally, she fell asleep, and I curled up right there in a corner near the wall and I fell asleep too.

The next thing I knew, I was awakened by a loud, evil voice. It was Mother again.

"Wake up, you little bitch, and pick up the floor!" Her eyes were so evil, all fake eyelashes and dark, snake-like eyes. She came at me again, this time hitting me across the head and ear. I felt a burning sensation. My ear was stinging so bad I could not help crying. But I was thankful she did not kick me. Immediately, I sectioned off my two inches again. She just went into the kitchen and filled up her glass. I could hear the ice cubes clank as they fell into her glass.

But then I could feel that Mother was close and looking at me. My hands started picking faster. I sat up straighter too in hopes of pleasing her. I knew what was next, and my stomach tightened. I could feel my throat close and my eyes squint tightly shut. Mother stomped over and kicked me in the stomach with her black pointed shoes again. It hurt so badly, but I knew there would be more, and then there was more and more over and over again. I could not breathe and held my stomach.

When relief finally came, a momentary end, I gasped for air as quietly as possible, the pain still lingering hard. I tried not to cry out loud, for if she heard me, she would become even angrier, and I just could not bear any more of her kicking.

Mother just laughed and said, "I will teach you little girl!"

I concentrated so hard on picking up the floor and thought so hard about how I wished Mother would like me. I would do the best job on the floor or rug and then she would be happy. I fantasized that she would be so happy about the job I did she would come over and tell me to stop and ask me what I wanted to eat and drink. Sometimes my mind would move in the other direction, and I would find myself wishing something bad would happen to her. I wished she would choke, but also wish

I was the only one who could save her and then wished that when I did save her, she would love me and never hurt me again.

I was so hungry, but I did not dare ask if Mother was planning on giving me something to eat. If I asked, she might not. Mother always read paperback books on the couch, and she ate there too. Sometimes she would ask me to take her dish to the kitchen, and when she did that, I would eat anything left on her plate, or would try and get whatever I saw lying around in the kitchen. If Father was going to be away for a long time, it would be days before I would get anything to eat.

The phone rang and Mother answered it, covering the phone with her hand and telling me to go into my room. Then she began talking. As I hurried towards my room, I could hear her talking. Then I just rushed into the bathroom and put my mouth up to the faucet and had a long drink and used the toilet.

I could still hear her talking. I knew it was her Mother on the phone. I knew because Mother always talked to her about me, calling me. "That little bitch." I peeked down the hallway to be sure it was safe and then quietly went in my room. I climbed into my bed, it felt so good, but my back was sore, and my knees were sore. My body was shaking. I felt so much pain and I was afraid to fall asleep so I would just cry a little and curl up and hug myself and rock back and forth and wish I could see my Grandmother and Grandfather. They would make everything all better. I could almost smell my Grandma's perfume and feel her holding me.

I was so hungry that my stomach was making noises. I did not mind because Mother wasn't in the room, and I would rather be hungry and left alone. Soon I fell asleep, but I woke up often to be sure where Mother was. The room was dark now, and it felt good to be able to fall asleep in my bed. I wasn't afraid of the dark at all—I was afraid of Mother.

****

The sunlight shone through the window, and I wished it would go away. I just lay there and wondered, *"When will my father come home?"* Things were so great when father was home. I could eat and drink all I wanted, and I did not have to pick up the floor. We would always go see Grandma and Grandpa, and sometimes I could stay there over night. These thoughts kept me calm and hopeful, and I clung to them as often and as much as I could.

I could hear some noise now. I just lay still, breathing quietly but with a staggering pull of air each time. I really enjoyed a deep breath that filled my lungs. Suddenly, the door opened and Mother came in the room. She glared at me and told me to get off the bed and onto the floor. She left the room and slammed the door shut. I could hear her in the kitchen. Then I heard her walking hard and fast back to my room. I saw the doorknob turn and the door swing open and I immediately looked at her feet to see if she had her pointed shoes on. When I saw she did not I was relieved. She never kicked me with her bare feet.

I kept my head low and stayed scrunched up against the wall. I knew she had something in her hand, but I was afraid to look. It could be a belt or a hairbrush or a spatula or a ruler or a yardstick or anything she had on hand that would sting and burn raw.

Mother threw a sandwich on the floor. I could smell the peanut butter. She just glared at me and swiftly left the room, slamming the door. I ate the sandwich. It was thick with peanut butter, but no jelly. I got really thirsty, but I knew I would not be getting a drink. I learned how to make my mouth water, and that helped me with the dry tickles in my throat.

I fell asleep after a while, and then suddenly again, the door flew open. Mother plodded over to me and hit me with a skinny black belt over and over again. It burned so badly, especially when she hit the same place twice. She told me to get up and go pick up the floor. I ran out and got down on my hands and knees again. My knees were still sore from before and even becoming raw. I sectioned off my two inches of rug once again and tried to concentrate on those two inches. I was in so much pain I could not stop shaking. Mother had this tall glass of something, and it looked so good. I could see the frosty water on the side of the glass and see the ice. I hoped she would leave the room, so maybe I could sneak just a little sip.

The phone rang again, and when Mother answered it, she started talking and waved for me to go to my room. I thought I could sneak to the bathroom again, but this time she watched me too closely. I hurried to the room and curled up on the floor, so she would not have to tell me to get off the bed again. In a few minutes, she walked in to check on me. I was so afraid that I looked up and just let it out again — "Can I go to the bathroom?"

She glared at me and said, "You have to go little girl, you go right there!" Then she went out. I just rocked and sat on the heel of my foot to hold it in for what seemed to be hours. It hurt so badly. She made me hold it in many times and would just watch and laugh at me. Finally, I had to go right away. I could not take it anymore. I saw a shirt in the corner of the room. I grabbed it and relieved myself on the floor in the shirt. The relief was so great I did not care what might happen next. I hid the mess in the shirt under the bed.

I went deep into thought about my grandparents; it helped me calm the scared, desperate feeling I had inside. I would concentrate on those good feelings and would take deep jerky breaths. Some would fill up my lungs and help me relax and think about how much they loved me and I loved them. I would daydream about living with them. It must have been hours that I just sat and daydreamed because I saw the sun was going down. I could not hear a sound, so I crept over to the door and opened it and looked down the hall. I had to go to the bathroom again. I grabbed the shirt under the bed and ever so softly went down the hallway to the bathroom. I put the shirt deep in the garbage can and sat on the edge of the toilet and went. I went to the sink and put my mouth under the faucet, I turned on the water very quietly and I drank so much I felt filled.

It was still quiet when I went down the hall to the kitchen. I knew Mother was out there, somewhere, but I hoped she was sleeping on the couch. I looked, and I could see her bare feet, lying very still. I went into the kitchen and found some bread on the counter. I took two pieces and found a cookie in the garbage. Then I hurried to the room. It was still so quiet. It was getting dark now. After I ate, my stomach felt better, but it was still sore. I just lay down on the bed and thought for a while until I fell asleep. I woke up in a state of terror before realizing it was okay. Mother was probably still sleeping. I went to the bathroom again, and drank some water, and she never heard me. Then I went back to sleep.

****

I felt heat and sensed light coming through the window. It felt good, but I did not like morning because I would rather sleep. I Knew Mother would not bother me when she was sleeping. I listened closely, so if I heard her I could get on the floor fast. I wasn't allowed to sleep in the bed unless Father was home. It was a long time before I heard any noise, and my stomach got so tight and my throat hurt. I lay there for a long time, probably hours, and then I heard another person. It was a voice I liked. It was Aunt J. She was always nice to me and told Mother to leave me alone. In a little while, I heard the door open. I got on the floor really fast, and I felt so sick. But it was Aunt J. She put her finger to her lips telling me to be quiet and asked me if I was okay. She'd brought me a sandwich and milk. I ate it quickly, drank the milk fast, and it was all really good. Then she told me she had to get out before Mother came and saw her there with me.

I was in that room for three days. Mother came in on the fourth day and told me I was bad, and that was why she had to teach me. She told me not to tell my father or anyone else, or she would really, really teach me. She told me to go into the bathroom and get in the bathtub. She made the water really hot and threw yellow soap into the tub and told me to scrub myself.

She told me to get on my knees and put my head under the water. She poured soap on my head and told me to scrub hard. I did everything she said. I rinsed my head, and she pushed me hard under the faucet. It scared me because the water was in my face and I could not breathe. I knew my Father was coming home because she kept telling me I was so bad and I'd better not say anything to him or she would teach me next time and also tell him how bad I was.

Mother got all dressed up. She put her black hair up in a bun and put her fake eyelashes on. She had me wear shorts and a shirt, and my hair was brushed too. I felt so happy inside that Father would be home. He was a good Father and I loved him so much. He had fights with Mother and would yell really loud and bang things too. I did not care because I could eat; drink, sleep, and play, and I knew we would visit my grandparents while he was home.

Father came in the door, and I jumped up and ran to him. He picked me up and hugged me so tight it hurt, and I let out a gasp of pain. He asked me what was wrong, but I just shut up and did not utter a word. He looked at Mother, but she went into the kitchen. Father put me down, and I went into my room to play with a doll Grandmother gave me. I could hear Father yelling really loud at Mother for a very long time.

"I WILL TEACH YOU LITTLE GIRL!"

CHAPTER TWO

My sister was born, and I thought she was awfully cute. She was very quiet for a baby. Mother's aunt and other family came over to help her take care of my baby sister. Mother would rest. She seemed distant from everything else. I was very happy because she would not bother with me any longer.

Father let me see my sister and touch her. One time she was holding my finger too tight, and I looked at Father and laughed. Mother turned and gave me that familiar look that scared me so much. She just came over and picked up my sister. Father did not notice what had happened, and I certainly would not tell him. Later, Father went to the store, and I asked if I could go too. Mother jumped in and started talking to him, so I wasn't noticed and could not go.

When he left, she put my sister in her crib and walked out where I was sitting and said, "You wait. I will teach you." I felt sick. I just froze and looked down at the floor. I wanted her to go away, but she just stood there glaring at me and said again "I will teach you, little girl!"

Soon, Father came home, and I felt better. We had dinner, and I ate and drank so much my father said I was a human garbage can, and I laughed. My sister was sleeping and Mother was being nice too for a change. I knew this wasn't real because she reminded me with that look of hers once in a while. I wished so hard that she would stay nice, but I knew that would not happen.

Father helped me get into bed and told me he had to go on a trip tomorrow, but he promised that when he came back, he would take me to Grandma and Grandpa's house for a visit. My throat felt sore and my stomach ached. I knew what was coming. Father hugged me and said everything would be all right. I wanted to tell him, "No! Don't go! She is going to hurt me again!" but I knew Mother would really hurt me if I said any such thing. I lay back and closed my eyes. I tried to think about going to my grandparents' house. This thought helped to force Mother out of my mind. It was so hard. I knew she was really going to hurt me again.

I woke up to a nasty pull of my hair. It was so fast I could not get my balance. The pulling grew tighter until I fell off the bed. Desperately, I tried to figure out which way to turn and what might be next. I looked up, but not at her face, I did not dare do that without permission.

Then she said, "Look at me, little girl! I will teach you to touch my baby, and who the hell do you think you are asking for a drink every minute? You won't have a drink today!" At that moment, she was so angry with me. She slapped my ear and my head. That hot, burning feeling on my ear was there again. It hurt so bad I had to grab my ear and cry out loud.

This noise made her even angrier, and she said, "I will teach you little girl! How many times do I have to tell you that children are to be seen and never heard!" I did not know what would come next. I just crouched down and tried to get ready. Mother pulled my hair and slapped me again. I had my ear turned away just right so she could hit only my head. That hurt, but not as bad as my ear. She mocked me by saying, "Oh, daddy can I sit on your lap? Oh, daddy, can I have a drink?"

Mother told me to get my little ass into the living room, so she could watch me. I went to the corner and held my legs and rocked. She sat on the couch and read her book. She always read books. This one had a picture of a beautiful lady with a long dress. Her hands were chained up and there was a man on a horse with a whip in his hand. I sat there for a long time, and then I heard someone was at the door. She told me to go to the bedroom. I liked it when people came over because Mother would stay away from me. I could sit and think of my grandparents. I would think of the fun we would have and how I could go to the bathroom and eat cookies. I was so hungry. I could hear my baby sister playing with mean Grand B. She did not like me, and she was very mean to me. She would tell my father I was so bad when he was gone. I went over to the corner of the room and knelt down, hugged my knees and rocked and hoped that they would not come in at all.

Suddenly the doorknob turned, and I started to panic and cry. Sometimes I just cried inside. I was so filled with fear. It was Grand B. She glared at me and then laughed and closed the door.

I heard her say, "Keep the little bitch in there." I was happy to stay in the room and not be out there where she would tell me I was no good. Grand B would tell me my real mother did not want me, and so they were stuck with me. I was a dirty brat and very bad. My real Grandmother always told me the word "brat" was a very bad word.

I was getting really thirsty, and I had to go to the bathroom. I decided to go to the door and look and see if I could sneak into the bathroom. I was shaking so much as I turned the doorknob. I turned it carefully and quietly. I knew if Mother saw me, I would be in big trouble. The doorknob was almost there... I started to pull open the door... I put my head out and I saw Mother standing there.

She screamed, "Where the hell do you think you are going, little girl?" and then I felt the door bang shut on my head. I felt stunned. It hurt, but I had to keep looking to see what was next. I started to speak and say I had to go to the bathroom, but I could not get the words out. Mother pushed me back in to the room and started slapping me saying, "I will teach you!"

I could not hold it in any longer and went to the bathroom. It went down my leg on to the floor and then she saw it. Mother really got mad then and started yelling at me, saying over and over again, "I will teach you little girl!"

She then went out of the room, but left the door open, and was still yelling at me. I knew she would be back with the belt. I went to the corner of the room and tried to cover myself with a shirt that was on the floor. She stormed into the room and just started hitting me again and again with the belt. I tried not to cry out loud, because this would make her get even angrier at me. It burned so bad, I tried to move away, but the belt just kept coming at me.

She was yelling and then she stopped and said in her evil voice that always scared me, "I will teach you little girl. I will tell you when you can pee. Now you sit in it!" She slammed the door and stomped away.

I was trembling and could not control my breathing and crying. I did not understand why Mother did not like me and always hurt me. My skin was burning so much. I cleared my eyes and wiped my nose and tried to take deep breaths. I just could not stop crying. I woke up later and saw it was dark outside the window. I could not hear anything at all, so I went back to sleep. I woke up again, and it was daytime. I was so thirsty, but I did not care. I just twisted my tongue down under where I could make moisture, and it helped me. I had red burning skin where the belt had hit me. It still burned.

THE MAN IN THE WINDOW

CHAPTER THREE

I had been staying with my grandparents more and more and I felt safe there. Grandfather and I went outside a lot, and I got to play with the kids that lived behind their house. I wished I never would have to leave and that Father would live there, too. I had a brother now, and I was going to go to school. I can remember I went to two schools, sometimes, from my grandparents' house and sometimes from my Father's house. Through the years I went to seven different elementary schools.

I heard a car in the driveway, and when I looked out the window, I saw Father get out of the car with Mother, my sister and my baby brother. They came inside, and Father gave me a hug and told me everything would be okay now.

I looked at Mother and she smiled at me. I liked it, but I was afraid anyway. I had stayed with my grandparents a lot. I had the feeling that Father had found out how mean Mother was to me when he was away. I had confused thoughts about it all. Why did Father always make me go home? Why couldn't I stay here, where I was safe and happy? Why couldn't my sister and brother stay here with me? I heard Father telling my grandparents it would all be okay now, and he would take me home where I belonged. They exchanged angry words and begged him to let me stay.

We went out to the car, and Father told me we were going home now. I felt a knot in my throat and started to cry, quietly at first and then loudly, calling out to my grandparents. They both waved and said "We love you," and Grandfather warned Father everything had better be okay and asked if he was sure it would be. Grandma was crying too, but trying to hold it back. Mother just stared out the window and did not look at anyone. We drove out of the drive way and beeped our horn three times as we did every time we left their house. I learned later on that the three honks meant, "I love you."

Father had to go on a trip again, and I could just feel it was a bad thing. I felt so sick I threw up outside and did not tell anyone. I wanted my Grandmother so badly. I missed her and my grandfather so much. Father said things would be okay and told me to be very good while he was gone and play with my sister. My sister called me "Sis" and she always wanted me to play with her. Mother would not let her around me very much, only if she wanted me to watch her. Mother would say I was dirty and told my sister to stay away from me. Mother's aunts and her mother came over a lot to see my baby brother and sister. My sister would cry to herself when Mother would hurt me. I would look at her and tell her after it was over, it was better to stay away from Mother right now.

Father was gone now, and Mother was not talking to me or looking at me. Her mother was there, and they were whispering to each other a lot. I knew it was about me, and I started to get scared. I hated having to call Mother's mom Grandmother. I was so afraid of her too. She got up to go home and gave me an evil look and took my brother and sister with her. My sister just looked at me with sad eyes.

Mother then looked at me and said, "I will fix you tonight." I went into my room and just kept wondering, *"What is she going to do to me?"* I could not think of anything else. I wanted my father and grandparents. Mother came into the room and told me to go eat. I made a mistake and sat at the table. I still don't know what I had done to make her so mad. I thought maybe it was because I should have sat on the floor in the corner to eat.

She moved towards me like a mad dog ready to attack and dragged me down to the floor and told me to pick up the floor and kicked me in the stomach, ribs and legs over and over. My arms took a lot of pain defending against her kicks. The familiar pain throbbed as usual, as I cried and caught my breath. I started to pick up the floor. I knew it would not be okay.

It was hours that I spent picking up the floor, and it was getting dark. Mother came over to me and said, "You will do this tonight," and she told me to go over near the wall and put a chair in front of me. The chair was turned around and the back faced me. She told me to pick the chair up and hold it up and straight out in front of me off the ground. If I dropped it, she would fix me. I knew that meant she would hurt me. I held the chair straight out, and it got so heavy I just could not do it. My arms hurt so much that I started to cry silently. The chair slid gently to the floor. I hoped Mother would not notice. I rested for just a few seconds and lifted it again.

I repeated this process a few times, and then my fears came true. Mother looked up right when the chair went to the floor. She looked at me with her evil snake black eyes, and I lifted the chair real high to try and make her happy. Mother did not come after me this time like I thought she would, so I just kept holding the chair until I just could not do so any more. The chair went down and Mother got up.

I picked the chair up quick, but she grabbed it out of my hands and said, "I will teach you little girl!" She then started hitting me with her hairbrush. Mother hit me over and over again with the brush. She did not kick me this time because she did not have her pointed shoes on. She told me if I dropped the chair again I would really get it.

I remember I was facing a large front window, and the couch where Mother was lying was to my right. She just lay down and started reading her book again while I held on to the chair with all my might. I had to go to the bathroom, but I knew I would have to hold it until Mother fell asleep. Then I would try and sneak to the bathroom if I felt I really had to go. The chair went down again, and Mother got up and hit me over and over on the same places she had hit me before. It hurt so bad I just cried and cried and begged to go to the bathroom.

She said, "If you pee, I will get the belt."

I fell down to that familiar position, kneeling on the heel of my foot and held it in to get control. I just could not hold it. I wasn't fast enough, so I kept saying, "I am so sorry — I am so sorry". I could feel the warmth and knew I would really get it now.

Mother turned and reached for the belt and just kept hitting me. I had my arms up and stayed huddled in the corner. When Mother stopped, I was so upset; I just kept crying and crying. She grabbed me by the hair and shoved my face into the puddle on the floor.

She was screaming at me, telling me "How do you like that little girl?" She then went in the other room for a few minutes, and I just tried to get my crying under control before she could come back and get mad again.

Mother came back and snapped at me to take the chair again. I grabbed the chair and held it up, and she went back to her book on the couch. I had wet pants and was shaking, but I was safe as long as the chair stayed up, and she had her book. I did not have to worry about sneaking off to the bathroom now, so I just tried to hold the chair up. I found a way to rest the chair on my leg, as I held it out, and this position helped me feel a little relief. Better yet, Mother did not seem to notice.

I kept holding the chair for what seemed like forever. Mother's eyes closed, and I put the chair down very slowly and rested, never taking my eyes off of Mother. I was so tired I just wanted to close my eyes. I tried to lean against the wall and close my eyes from time to time. I would jerk when I was about to fall, and that would help me stay awake and check on Mother. It

36

became routine most nights, until one night I saw a man in the window just staring at me. I was so afraid, but I did not dare wake Mother because I was more afraid of her and what she would do to me than the man in the window. This man just kept staring at me, and he smiled. For some reason it comforted me even though it scared me too.

Mother woke up briefly and looked over to make sure I was holding the chair. I saw her move and held the chair up in front of me. I was tired, and my body was sore, but that was okay as long as Mother kept sleeping. When I looked at the window again, the man was not there anymore.

"YOU ARE SO DIRTY!"

CHAPTER FOUR

When I was in my room for days at a time, I would have to go to the bathroom in the corner of the room. I would be fed on the floor and not allowed to take a bath or clean up. I remember Mother was very angry with me one morning and came in the room and screamed at me and kicked me over and over again. She was mad because I went to the bathroom in the corner of the room on the floor and tried to hide it in a t-shirt. She to grabbed me by the hair and rubbed my face in the mess I had made, and it was so bad. Some of it went into my mouth and nose. I was so upset that I just cried and cried. I thought I would throw up, but as I started to gag, she told me if I did throw up she would make me eat that, too. Mother got some of the mess on her and ran to the bathroom. I can remember she did not like things that smelled bad, or bugs or any other creatures.

Mother left me alone in the room for a long time, until it got dark and then light again. I cleaned off my face and went to the corner against the wall and grabbed my knees and rocked myself to sleep. I was shaking and had hard time breathing. After a while I closed my eyes and fell asleep.

I was awakened when I heard Mother's voice talking to my sister and brother. I knew she would be coming soon, and I was really afraid. My hair and body smelled so bad, and I still felt sick to my stomach. I had not had anything to eat or drink for three days, so my stomach hurt too, and my mouth was very dry. I was afraid to move or even think of asking for a drink. I remember thinking how the monster that was Mother would come any minute and hurt me again. I started sobbing and wished my father would come home and see what Mother did. I daydreamed about my Father coming home and catching her hurting me. The doorknob turned, and my stomach went stiff and my throat felt so sore.

Mother walked in and said, "Get in the bathroom, little girl. You are so dirty."

I was afraid to pass by her; I just could not take another kick. I got up and could feel my whole body shaking and shaking. I kept my head down and moved past her as fast as I could and ran into the bathroom. Mother came in and ran the bath water. I could see the steam coming up, and I knew it would be awful hot. I began to cry silently because I knew what was going to happen. Mother grabbed my arm and told me to get into the bathtub. I put my foot in, and she pushed me the rest of the way. The water was hot, but not as bad as the last time when my body had turned red, and my Father had become very angry.

Mother told me I was a dirty brat and very bad. She put bleach in the water and threw the yellow soap at me and told me to scrub myself good, or otherwise she would do it for me. I began to scrub all over until I was sure I had all the dirt and smell off. The smell of the bleach was making me sick. The water was getting cold too, but I did not care. I just wanted to stay there and be left alone.

I turned on the water just enough to let the water trickle into my mouth. It felt good to get a drink of water. It had been dark three times since I had a drink. I was very hungry too. I was thinking that my father might be coming home soon, because when I got a bath it was usually because he was coming home or someone was coming over. Sometimes I would not get a bath for weeks otherwise.

Mother came in and told me to let the water drain out of the tub. I did, and she told me to get on my knees and put my head under the water coming from the faucet. She held my head under so long; I could not breathe, and I choked. Mother told me to wash my hair and kept pushing my head under the faucet, banging my head into the wall and metal faucet. I kept trying to breathe when I had the chance and keep my balance.

She threw me a towel and called me some really bad names and said I was very bad. She told me I had better keep my mouth shut, or she would shut it for me. I knew this meant not to tell my Father or anyone else. She gave me clothes to wear, and I put them on fast and went to my room. Mother gave me a towel and told me to clean up my mess and that I was a little pig and so dirty. She left the room, and I started cleaning up the smelly mess. Mother then came in the room with a bucket of soapy water and told me to scrub the floor. I scrubbed and then wiped the floor with the towel. After a while Mother came in and told me to take the bucket outside and empty it and then get back in the house and pick up the floor.

I went outside and emptied the bucket. There I saw a neighbor lady outside too. She looked at me and smiled. I could not smile back because I was just too sad. I went back into the house and went to the living room where my sister and brother were watching TV. I started to pick up the floor again. Mother, however, soon got us all in the car. I felt so good and happy because I was sure my father was coming home. When Mother started driving, I noticed we were not heading to get Father the way we always did.

Soon it was clear we were going to her mother's house, and I felt sick inside again. If her father was there, it would be better because they would not be as mean to me. He did not let them hit me. He would get very mad at them. We pulled in the yard. It was a big yard, and the house was white and built high with steps going up. I later found out her father had built the house. I saw his car and was relieved. We got out of the car, and the neighbor lady across the street came over to say hello and then asked what was wrong with me. I thought I would just cry right there, in the hope that the lady would rescue me. I controlled myself; however, knowing it would be worse on me if I reacted. Mother just told the lady, "Oh she has been so bad today". The lady only looked at me and smiled. To this day I wonder what she really thought. I had marks all over me and a fat lip. The neighbor lady just went back into her house across the street.

We all started up the stairs, and Mother told me to go sit under the tree in the yard. I liked that even if I had to sit there for hours; it was safer than in the house. I could watch the ants make their home in the pile of sand and carry crumbs there and wish I could join them. I would think about being with them in their house and how happy I would be with them. As time passed, I heard my two sisters and brother playing inside. I liked hearing that they were having fun. I loved them so much. My new baby sister was so cute. I knew if they could stop Mother from hurting me they would, but they were too little. I thought they must feel very confused.

SNUGGLED AND SAFE

CHAPTER FIVE

Every time Father would come home, he would get angry and knock down Mother's hobby, her ceramics, and yell at her. I could tell the argument was about me. Part of me was glad, but another part knew I would pay dearly the next time Father went on a trip. As usual, right after the fight we would go to my grandparents' house. Father and Grandfather would go outside, and I would hug Grandmother as hard as I could. I would cry, but soon I would feel safe; and my heart would pound with happiness. It was a feeling that filled my whole self and overflowed into my soul and every part of my being giving me a warm safe feeling. Throughout my whole life, I felt this way about my grandparents, and I know that is what kept me sane and able to bear the pain each time my monster mother attacked me.

Grandmother has told me that one time when I came to stay with her I had a bubble bath and when she tucked me in bed, I snuggled up and said, "Grandma I feel like a real princess." I can remember feeling so snug with the soft pillow and sheets and blanket all around me. Sometimes I still think about the time and feel that snug same feeling.

It was such a treat to stay at my grandparents' house. I could eat and drink when I wanted to. We would sit at the table and eat together. I would help Grandmother make cookies and help Grandfather cut the grass on his riding mower. My Grandfather had beehives, and he would let me watch him from the window, as he gathered the honey. He would dress up in his protected outfit, and looked just like a spaceman. He would let me try the honey and chew on the wax.

I also had friends in the house behind their house, and we would play for hours during the day. I was able to put all the bad thoughts away and not think about them. My Grandmother would take me to church every Sunday, and to Sunday school. One of my sisters would come sometimes and stay with us, too; we had so much fun together. I loved my sisters and brother very much.

I went to elementary school right up the street. It felt normal and happy there. I think my teachers knew what was going on and why I attended school off and on. One teacher was really nice to me and told me not to worry and that my grandparents loved me so very much. I wanted to tell her how really mean Mother was, and that I never wanted to go back to live with her, but my grandparents said it was our family business, and we should not talk about it.

Then it all would happen again. Father would come and get me, and I would go to another school. He would go on a trip, and Mother would start in again.

****

My father told me I would be fine and belonged at home with Mother and the family. I did miss him, but I wished he would live at my

Grandparents house instead. I can remember not having a drink unless I was at school or when I could sneak to the back of the house and turn on the outside faucet and get a drink.

As I got older, I had more chores to do — scrubbing the bathroom, floors, walls, and steps for hours at a time. The only time I could stop was when Mother had company. She would send me outside with the dogs. I loved being with the dogs; I would play house and make them mud pies. They were collies, and their names were Cindy and Lancer. I would have to sleep outside with them at times, but I felt safe with them. When I was hungry enough, I would even eat their food.

I was in another world outside until Mother called me in again. Then the pain would start again and the fear would return. I would usually go straight down on my knees immediately to pick up the floor. Mother would walk over and look at me like nothing was going to happen, and then she would kick me in the ribs. If she could not get me in the ribs or stomach, she would kick my shins.

THE RIDE TO DOC'S

CHAPTER SIX

Once I actually scrubbed the kitchen floor from morning to lunchtime, Mother screamed for me to go outside and that she did not want to look at me. I was so happy, but did not dare let her know. I ran to the side of the house and hugged Cindy and Lancer, and they snuggled close to me. I think they knew what I was going through. I leaned on the side of the house and relaxed. I would daydream and go into another world. I had lots of worlds I could enter. Sometimes I would just sit there and wonder if my real Mother would be so mean and where she was. My grandparents told me she been nice.

This day would not be so calm and filled with daydreams. Mother screamed for me to stand up. I was just in my underwear bottoms with no shirt on as usual. I was not allowed to get dressed, but no one could see me in the house or yard. I was very self-conscious about anyone seeing my body. I always would try and put my arms in front of my breasts. Mother said for me to go get my bike. I brought it over to her, and she said I had to go to Doc's to buy her a pack of cigarettes. I turned and started to go toward the house to get dressed.

Mother screamed to me to get back here. I came back, and she said, "Where do you think you are going, little girl" I did not understand. I said to get dressed to go to the store. She gave me this real evil look and told me to get my little ass on the bike without any clothes. I just froze. I said very carefully that I needed my clothes and that I would hurry. She then slapped me. My lip was bleeding I could taste it.

She said, "Get your little ass on that bike!" I can remember that feeling. I just kept crying and begging her to let me get dressed. She gave me the money and I balled it up in my hand. Crying and trembling, I got on the bike and started to ride up the street. I was half way down the block when some kids started to laugh at me. I was so terrified and embarrassed that I just went faster. I was crying so hard I almost could not see where I was going. I felt so sick I thought I might throw-up. I thought I saw a car next to me driving very slowly. I looked over and wiped my eyes and saw Mother driving the car. She was laughing at me. I just kept going, crying all the way to Doc's drug store.

When I got there, I went in, and Doc was at the counter. I tried to talk, but it was so hard I took a deep breath and told him what I needed.

He just stared at me with a very confused look and said, "Are you all right there?" I nodded yes and he said, "You should have some clothes on. Where are your Mother and Father?" I said' "In the car" and walked out. I was crying a little less, but still humiliated. I held the cigarettes tight and started to ride back home. I knew Mother was there right by me, but I did not care, I was just so worried about those same kids seeing me again. As I got closer to where they were before, I did not see them so I just peddled home as fast as I could.

I went to Mother and gave her the cigarettes, and she laughed at me. I gave her the first dirty look I had ever given her and ran to Cindy and Lancer on the side of the house. I thought she would be after me, but she went in the house. I cried for a while, and then I just sat there and wished she would get hurt and have to stay away forever. I wished Doc had helped me. I wished the neighbors or those kids had helped me.

My lip was sore, and I could still taste the salty, dried blood. It hurt, but I had not felt it until now. My body was really sore, and I felt like I never felt before. I felt good because I have given Mother a dirty look. I felt a brave rage rising inside me that I never had felt before. If it wasn't summer and I was still going to school, I think I would have told my teacher what was happening. This was the first time I ever felt like standing up to Mother. I felt like I was being seen and heard.

This feeling was soon to be over when Mother called me.

A NIGHT IN THE BUSHES

CHAPTER SEVEN

Father was on a trip, and as usual, I was cleaning and cleaning. I really did not mind cleaning, as it would let me daydream and take me away. I wanted to sleep most nights; but I had to pick up the floor all night. By this time, I was always put to work cleaning anything and everything, and if it wasn't done right, I would get beat and have to start all over again.

This time, I had to scrub the kitchen floor and the steps outside at the back of the house. It took most of the day. I noticed the neighbor looking over at me from time to time. I just glanced up and kept scrubbing. When I would scrub, I would do it in sections because I knew I would be there a long time. One day I was daydreaming that I was in a store, and I heard a lady talking about her little girl and that she had come from England to find her. I ran up and said my name to her, and she scooped me up and hugged me tight and said, "I am your Mum."

****

Mother came outside right then and said, "Get in the house and pick up the floor." I went in and started sectioning it off inch by inch. Mother came over and said to stand up. I did, and she kicked me in the shin. I fell down, and she just kept kicking me and calling me a little bitch.

"I will teach you, little bitch!" she said. Her hand hit my ear and face over and over again. My brother and two sisters were on the couch and stayed very quiet. They just looked at the TV or out the window. She never beat them like me, but she did hit them with hairbrushes or spatulas or whatever was on hand at the time when she got mad at them.

This day was unlike most others. Mother was really in a rage, and she just kept on and on. After taking as much as I could, I got up and ran to the door. I barely got out and away from her and ran down the street. I looked back and saw Mother wasn't after me. I ran to a neighbor's house across the road and a little ways down the street. I yelled for help as I cried and banged on the door.

The lady came and asked me what was wrong, I was sobbing and shaking, but I also felt something inside that was almost a righteous feeling. I felt like I was finally doing what I needed to do. I begged the lady to please help me and that my Mother was beating me and I needed help.

The lady said, "I can't get involved, Go home now," and closed the metal flip blinds on her door. My heart just fell. I could hardly breathe. I begged again and then realized she was not going to help me. I could not go back home.

I took a deep breath and decided to run away. I looked around and did not see Mother anywhere, so I just started running down the street. I knew that my father was coming home soon, so I decided to hide in the bushes on a corner near the street until I saw his car, no matter how long it took. It was getting dark, but I felt safe anyway. I just took the familiar position of sitting and hugging my knees and rocked and rocked.

I felt so tired and also a little afraid of the dark, but there was a light post nearby, so I did have some light. I hoped my father would come home tomorrow, but I did not care, I knew I could not go back, and I would have to wait. I fell asleep until the warm sun woke me. I looked around and hoped my father would be there soon. I stayed in the bushes waiting, and it seemed like forever. I did not care if I had to stay there forever because, I felt safe.

I looked up and saw my Father's car. I jumped up scratching myself on the bushes. I jumped in front of my Father's car.

He slammed on the brakes in shock, jumped out and scooped me up and said, "Not again".

He put me in the car and took me to one of my friend's houses and asked my friend's Mom to please let him bathe me and figure out what to do next. I told him everything. This was the first time someone else was involved outside the family. He told me to stay with my friend overnight. I was very happy, but I wanted him to stay too. He told my friends' mother that he was going to pretend that he knew nothing and see what would happen.

The next day my father picked me up and took me to my grandparents' house. I again stayed there for a very long time.

Father told me once again, "Everything will be Okay."

****

It was morning, and I was in my room on the floor, sitting quietly, listening for Mother to yell for me or barge in screaming. I heard her in the kitchen getting coffee. I was in my underwear bottoms sitting in the corner on the floor. I had to go to the bathroom, so I waited until I was almost sure Mother was on the couch. I opened the door very slowly and looked down the hall. I did not see Mother, so I made it into the bathroom and sat way up towards the front of the seat so I could go without making noise.

Suddenly, the door flew open, and Mother stared down at me hard and cold. She screamed, "Who do you think you are, little girl? You did not ask me to come in here!"

I tried to utter, "I had to go".

Mother looked at me with her evil eyes and grabbed my arm. Again in an evil voice, she said, "I will fix you little girl!" She twisted me around and grabbed my hair and pushed my head into the toilet. She said, "I will teach you!" I was shaking and thinking, *please stop*. I held my breath, but she just kept pushing and holding me down. I did not think I could hold my breath much longer when she flushed the toilet and pulled me up.

Mother grabbed me by the neck and pushed me into the room and down onto the floor. At this point, I was just trying to keep my balance as I hit the wall and then the floor. I was trembling, but watching Mother closely. I was afraid she would start kicking me.

Mother turned and went out and slammed the door. I took a shirt from the corner and wiped my face. I sat under the window and grabbed my legs and rocked for what seemed to be hours, but I was glad to be alone. I fell asleep waking up every few minutes with a jerk as my arms would let go of my legs.

Mother then yelled, "Get your little ass out here!"

I hurried out of the room. She told me to take out the garbage and clean up the outside. I did not have a shirt on, and I knew not to ask to get dressed. I would cross my arms and tuck my hands under my arms to cover up.

When Mother saw this, she said, "Put your arms down, little girl." I would let them fall to my side.

Cleaning up the garbage took hours with Mother always inspecting. If she found one piece on the ground, dumping the rest out and telling me to start over was no surprise. I carried the garbage out to the side of the house and started picking up the trash that Mother had strewn all over. I made sure I looked between the grass blades to make sure every section was perfect.

After a while Mother came out and said, "Pick it up!" She emptied one of the bags again.

I started again. As I did, a man's voice said, "Are you okay?" It scared me. I looked up and stepped back. Then I hurried and crossed my arms to hide myself. I did not answer him, but I wanted to. I wanted to say, "Please help me." The man walked away, but he kept turning back to look at me. I felt sick and went over to the side of the house to vomit. Nothing would come up. I just kept gagging. I went back over and started picking up the trash again. I would check every section just like I did when I would pick up the floor.

My mind would drift into thoughts, and unlike when I was younger, when I wanted Mother to like me, I now pictured her hurt and begging me to help her, and then I saw me reaching out and helping her, and her being sorry for ever hurting me. I thought her getting hurt, and knowing she would be gone and never able to hurt me again. She became an evil monster, and I just thought bad things that could happen to her. I hated her so much... but I feared her even more.

THE VOICE IN THE DARKNESS

CHAPTER EIGHT

At night, when I was curled up in bed or on the floor in the corner, it was so quiet that I was almost sure I was safe until the morning light came through the window. I would listen to the silence and just rock back and forth. Some nights I would hear noises outside and see shadows. It scared me, but I never dared move or go for help. I was more afraid of Mother than what was outside. I would sit frozen and watch and listen.

The shadows would get closer and bang the window, and a crackling evil monster voice would say, "I'm going to get you!" and "I am coming to get you!" I just wished that the monster would come in the house and get Mother.

The same event kept happening at night and very frequently, and it really scared me. I would just stay quiet until the monster went away, and then I would rock myself to sleep. These visits from the evil monster went on for years. The monster would even come when Father was home from work. It would be time for bed, and we would all be in our beds. I was allowed to sleep in bed when Father was there, and it felt so good to be able to go to sleep and not worry about Mother coming in to hurt me.

Then I would wake up with the bang at the window. It would be dark, and everyone was sleeping. I would see shadows at the window, and the evil monster would cackle its words once again.

"I'm going to get you!" and "I am coming to get you!" Maybe the Monster is Mother...

****

I did escape the Monster, and every day I get stronger.

The abuse will never be forgotten and in this case never forgiven; why would it be?

Child abuse is a profoundly chilling part of our society. Children are helpless at the mercy of the adults around them, children cannot help themselves. Some children are terrified of speaking out, while others actually think they are bad and this is a normal punishment. What is more disturbing is the fact that family members and friends of the family witness the abuse inflicted on the child and avoid getting involved. We all need to reach in our hearts and get involved.

Survivors of child abuse in most cases share the same link in life; trying to move on and proclaim a normal life. In conversations with abused survivors; unfortunately the trauma of the abuse lives on and in some cases it drains their spirit and emotions of every aspect of their lives.

CPSIA information can be obtained at www.ICGtesting.com
Printed in the USA
LVOW10s2223150913

352566LV00002B/400/P